Dominic Kampshoff

Basics Sound Protection

Dominic Kampshoff

Basics Sound Protection

BIRKHÄUSER
BASEL

Contents

Foreword

In urban environments and places with a lot of technical equipment, people are constantly exposed to sounds and noise. This can have a negative effect on health. In rooms living or work spaces, it is particularly important to minimize unwanted noises and to ensure that the acoustics are agreeable.

Sound protection not only relates to the acoustic requirements to be met by building components, but it also includes the acoustic surface properties in rooms. The effect of sound emissions is directly affected by urban structures, the layout of buildings, the construction of building components, and, often, the installations in buildings. Good acoustics design helps to reduce the immission of noise from the outside and also contributes to the usability of spaces, such as auditoria and open-plan offices, which directly relates to the well-being of their users.

When taking these guiding principles into account at the design stage, it is necessary to be well informed about sound protection requirements and the options for achieving it. In addition to familiarity with building construction details, this requires an understanding of the physics of acoustics and the measures available to deal with sound-related problems. An understanding of sound protection is as an integral part of the design process. To this end, *Basics Sound Protection* provides a comprehensive introduction that enables readers to carry out their own design work with a thorough understanding of the issues involved.

Bert Bielefeld
Editor

Introduction

Sound protection is part of building physics and is an important subject in the design of buildings and structures. In practice, this means that suitable solutions have to be worked out for acoustic problems, ensuring that they do not interfere with other aspects (such as structural aspects, thermal building physics, and fire safety requirements). Sound protection can be roughly divided into sound immission protection, building acoustics, and room acoustics.

Sound immission protection is concerned with sound impacting on a building from the outside, for example from road or rail traffic, industrial and commercial facilities, port activities, underground parking garages, and leisure facilities. In areas subject to high noise levels, it is particularly important to take into account the sound immissions affecting the building to be designed because this is the basis for construction-related sound protection of external building components and can lead to fundamental decisions regarding the orientation and plan layout of the building. > Chapter Sound immission protection

Building acoustics deals with the sound protection of a building. The idea here is to protect rooms from the impact of noise, both from the outside and from sounds emanating from other rooms in the building or from building services installations. In this context, it is important to note that the more the building is protected against noise from the outside, the more acutely internal noises will be perceived. When designing internal sound protection, the actual function of the respective room should always be considered as a priority. The most important task in the design process is the determination of the sound attenuation properties of components, both in terms of calculations and measurements. To be able to do this, architects have to have basic knowledge of acoustics, of the sound transmission paths, and of the sound insulation properties of materials and building components. > Chapter Building acoustics

In room acoustics, the engineer strives to optimize the audibility in a room. Depending on the function of the room, this means achieving optimum audibility of the spoken word or optimum acoustic quality for musical performances. However, in room acoustics, the subject of noise protection will often also play a role, for example where the room in question is close to noisy industrial and commercial premises or is in a day nursery or school. In these cases, it is possible to lower the noise level with specific room acoustics measures. Architects and specialist engineers dealing with this subject need to be familiar with sound propagation within rooms and the acoustic properties of building materials and their placement within the room. In view of the fact that room acoustics measures usually have a major impact on the interior design and the surfaces within the room, such measures should be considered at an early stage in the design process. > Chapter Room acoustics

In this volume, we will first explain the basics of acoustics. We will explain basic terms of physics, how sound is created and propagated, and how sound is perceived by the human ear. In the chapter on sound immission protection, we explain how sound immission is assessed, and we provide examples of how noise can be attenuated and what design options are available.

In the chapters on building acoustics and room acoustics, the reader is familiarized with the respective key variables and how sound propagates within rooms and within the building structure. In addition, the effects of the geometry of rooms, of the construction of components, and of materials on the acoustic design are discussed.

In this volume, we are not directly covering the calculation of sound protection as required by the standards; readers should refer to the respective national standards and regulations. Instead, the intention is to convey to the reader a basic understanding of sound-related requirements in design and construction.

Fundamentals of acoustics

Sound protection may play an important role as early as the design stage of a project because it may influence the orientation of a building and its plan layout. Noise to be considered is that impacting on the building from the outside, as well as that generated inside the building, i.e., noise caused by people or technical installations. When, at an early design stage, a building is oriented such that the effect of external noise is minimized and the plan layout makes sense in terms of noise attenuation, it may be possible to significantly simplify future design input and may also lead to a reduction in the cost of construction. The calculations and the assessment of noise impacting on the building, and the construction detailing, are normally carried out by a building physics or acoustics engineer. Close cooperation between architects, clients, and specialist engineers is an important prerequisite for a successful overall design. A certain basic knowledge of physics is needed for a person to be able to determine and assess the impact of noise at the facade of a building, to design the details of building components to ensure that they meet sound-related requirements, and to design the geometry and surfaces of a room in accordance with room acoustics requirements. The most important aspects are explained below.

KEY VARIABLES IN PHYSICS

The term "sound" refers to mechanical vibrations in a gaseous, liquid, or solid substance. These vibrations lead to particles compacting and decompacting. The speed of the moving particles (molecules) is referred to as <u>sound particle velocity</u>. The propagation speed of sound depends on the medium and on the temperature within that medium. > Fig. 1, Table 1

Sound, sound particle velocity, speed of sound

Particle compaction = maximum pressure

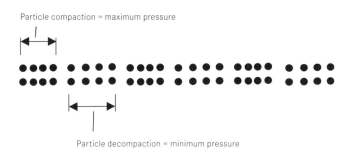

Particle decompaction = minimum pressure

Fig. 1: Particles compacting and decompacting

Table 1: Speed of sound in different media

Medium	Speed of sound [m/s]
Air (20°C)	approx. 343
Steel	up to about 5,800
Masonry	approx. 2,600–4,000
Reinforced concrete	approx. 3,300–4,900
Timber/wood	up to about 5,800
Glass	approx. 4,000–5,500

Frequency   When assessing sound, frequencies play an important role. The frequency f refers to the number of vibrations per second. As the frequency increases, so does the pitch. The frequency is stated in hertz [1/s]. For the acoustician, it is important to know which frequencies are the determining factor in the assessment of, for example, the construction of components. The sound level is frequently stated as an octave or one-third frequency band. > Fig. 2

Wavelength   Depending on the speed of sound of the medium and the frequency or time period, it is possible to calculate the wavelength λ. Depending on the medium and frequency, this can vary a great deal, which means that determining the wavelength is a mandatory requirement for designing acoustics measures. > Fig. 3

$$\lambda = \frac{c}{f} \ [m]$$

whereby:
c = speed of sound in m/s
f = frequency in Hz

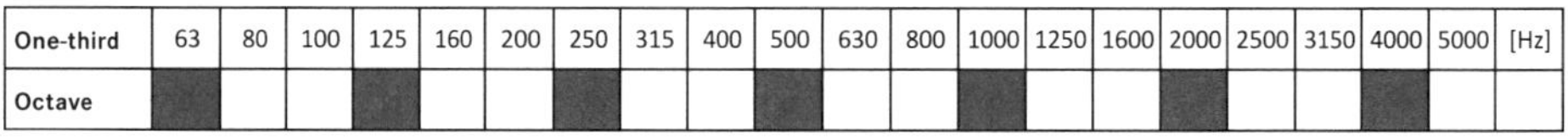

One-third	63	80	100	125	160	200	250	315	400	500	630	800	1000	1250	1600	2000	2500	3150	4000	5000	[Hz]
Octave	■			■			■			■			■			■			■		

Fig. 2: Diagram illustrating one-third and octave frequency bands

○ **Note**: The doubling of vibrations is referred to as an octave; one octave is equivalent to three one-thirds.

● **Example**: Sound propagating in air with a speed of sound of approx. 343 m/s and a frequency of 200 Hz has a wavelength of approx. 1.7 m. If the frequency is increased to 2,000 Hz, the wavelength is significantly reduced to approx. 0.17 m.

Fig. 3: Wavelength λ

The human ear can perceive frequencies of between 16 Hz and 20,000 Hz. Frequencies below 16 Hz are referred to as infrasound and those above 20,000 Hz as ultrasound. Depending on the discipline, acousticians define different frequency ranges when making acoustics assessments. > Fig. 4

In acoustics, a distinction is made between tone, complex tonal sound, and noise. Tone is an audio signal with uniform and regular vibrations. An example is the tone generated by a tuning fork. Complex tonal sound consists of several superposed frequencies. For these frequencies to generate a complex tonal sound, the ratio of one to the other must be a whole-number one. Where the ratio of one frequency to another is not a whole-number one and the frequencies are not identical, the resulting sound is called noise. > Fig. 5

In order to be able to determine and assess sound in practice, the key acoustics variables sound pressure p and sound pressure level L_p are used. For example, when talking we produce variations in pressure that superpose with the pressure of the air around us. In this process, the molecules in the air (mostly oxygen and nitrogen) are excited. The pressure thus created is passed on to the neighbouring molecules, which results in areas with greater and lesser pressure. These differences in

Tone, complex tonal sound, noise

Sound pressure, sound pressure level, sound power level

Infrasound	→	< 16 Hz
Audible range	→	16 Hz bis 20,000 Hz
Music	→	16 Hz bis 160,000 Hz
Speech	→	63 Hz bis 8,000 Hz
Room acoustics	→	63 Hz bis 4,000 Hz
Building acoustics	→	100 Hz bis 5,000 Hz
Techn. noise abatement	→	50 Hz bis 10,000 Hz
Ultrasound	→	> 20,000 Hz

Fig. 4: The different frequency ranges considered by the different acoustics disciplines

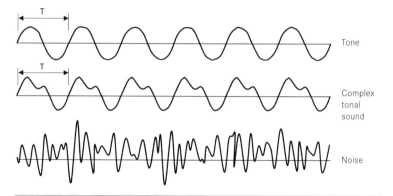

Fig. 5: Tone, complex tonal sound, and noise

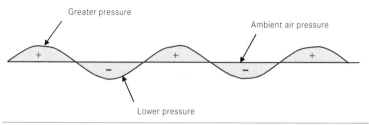

Fig. 6: Differences in pressure compared to the surrounding air pressure

pressure spread out in a wave-like motion. Sound pressure is stated in
pascals [Pa]. > Fig. 6

Compared to the surrounding air pressure, the variations in pressure
generated are very small. As a comparison, the surrounding air pressure
is approx. 100,000 Pa, whereas the pressure differentials that can be perceived by the human ear are between 0.00002 and 20 Pa. For this reason, the key variable used in acoustics is not sound pressure but the log-
arithmic variable, the sound pressure level.

○ **Note:** Sound pressure is calculated using the force
acting on the air molecules in relation to the area.
The louder we speak, the greater the force. If the area
is the same, the sound pressure p will be greater.

$$p = \frac{F}{A} [Pa]; \quad F = \text{force [N]}; \quad A = \text{area}$$

○ **Note:** Formula for the sound pressure level:

$$L_p = 20 \lg \frac{p}{p_0} \ [dB]$$

p_0 refers to the lower audible threshold of 0.00002 Pa;
in the upper audible range, say 20 Pa, the sound pressure level is 120 dB.

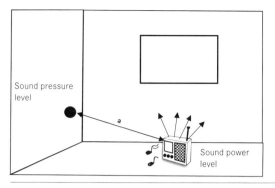

Fig. 7: Sound pressure level and sound power level

If the ventilation plant of a building is to be installed in the open or on the roof, it is important to check the effect this has on neighbouring buildings. As a rule, the manufacturers of such equipment are able to state the sound level. In this case, it is important to note whether the value stated is the <u>sound pressure level L_p</u> or the <u>sound power level L_w</u>. The sound power level is the sound power emitted by the respective equipment, which always remains constant. By contrast, the sound pressure level varies according to distance: the farther away one is from the equipment, the lower the level. For this reason, it is imperative that information given about the sound pressure level includes the distance at which it was measured. > Fig. 7

In practice, it is often necessary to add or subtract several sound levels from each other. Unfortunately, it is not possible to add or subtract sound pressure levels; instead, this has to be done logarithmically, i.e., sound energy must be used.

Calculating with sound levels

The following rules apply:

●

Addition of different sound levels L_k

$$L_{total} = 10 \lg \sum_{k=1}^{n} 10^{\frac{L_k}{10}} \quad [dB]$$

● **Example**: The following can help to give an idea of how sound levels change:
– Addition of *two* identical sound levels results in a sound level increase of *3 dB*
– Addition of *three* identical sound levels results in a sound level increase of *5 dB*
– Addition of *ten* identical sound levels results in a sound level increase of *10 dB*

Table 2: Subjective perception of changes in sound levels

Sound level change	Subjective perception
1 dB	hardly audible
3 dB	clearly audible
10 dB	twice as loud or half as loud

Addition of identical sound levels L_k

$$L_{total} = L_k + 10 \lg n \quad [dB]$$

It is often necessary to find out by how much the sound level has changed. This may be as a result of a new building or changes in transport infrastructure (road, rail, etc.). In order to be better able to estimate changes in sound levels, it is possible to assume typical subjective perceptions. > Table 2

SOUND PROPAGATION

Sound waves

Sound is created by a vibrating body exciting air particles (air molecules) and propagating them in a wave-like motion. A distinction is made between the vibrating movement in the direction of propagation (longitudinal waves), the movement perpendicular to the direction of propagation (transverse waves), and air molecules that turn in the direction of propagation (bending waves). > Fig. 8

If the molecules excited by the variations in pressure move in the direction of propagation, this is referred to as longitudinal waves. These types of waves are the only ones occurring in air.

In liquids or solid bodies, particles can also vibrate perpendicular to the direction of propagation in the form of transverse waves. Bending waves, on the other hand, are prominent in board-shaped components (e.g., plasterboard, wood-based board, etc.) because, in these components, the vibrating movement in the direction of propagation is combined with a turning movement of the solid particles of the excited board.

○ > Chapter Building acoustics

○ **Note**: The reason why only longitudinal waves can occur in sound propagation in air is that air has no shear rigidity or flexural rigidity.

○ **Note**: In order to be able to propagate, sound waves always need a medium (air, steel, concrete, etc.). In contrast to electromagnetic waves (light waves, radio waves, etc.), sound waves can't propagate in a space void of air.

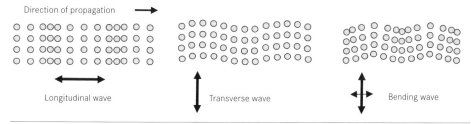

Direction of propagation →

Longitudinal wave

Transverse wave

Bending wave

Fig. 8: Direction of sound propagation

When designing a building, it is often important to ascertain the amount of noise the planned building will be exposed to from sources in the surroundings, such as transport infrastructure and commercial facilities. Conversely, for example, in the case of commercial buildings, it may be necessary to assess the sound-related effects of the planned building on the surroundings. This may involve checking the effects of a ventilation plant, combined heat and power stations, entrances to underground parking garages, delivery traffic, outside eateries, and commercial or industrial equipment. Likewise, civil engineering projects such as roads, tunnels, and bridges may have to be checked for their noise impact on the surroundings. In order to carry out the respective calculations and assessment, it is necessary to be familiar with how sound propagates in the open and how the propagation of sound is affected.

Sound propagation in the open

The attenuation of <u>sound propagation in the open</u> (reduction in the sound level) is primarily affected by the respective distances and by the geometric shape of the sound wave. However, sound-screening and sound-reflecting objects and building components, as well as meteorological influences, also have a significant effect on the sound level and have to be taken into account in the acoustics assessment.

The sound level decreases with the increasing distance from the sound source. For example, in the case of a road, which can be considered a linear source of noise, doubling the distance leads to a sound level reduction of approx. 3 dB. In the case of a heat pump, which owing to its geometry can be considered as a point source of noise, doubling the distance leads to a sound level reduction of approx. 6 dB.

Attenuation by distance

However, when assessing the source of noise, it is necessary to take into account its location. For example, if the heat pump is located directly in front of a house wall, it is necessary to take into account the sound reflections via the house wall and the ground in addition to the direct sound transmission. > Fig. 9

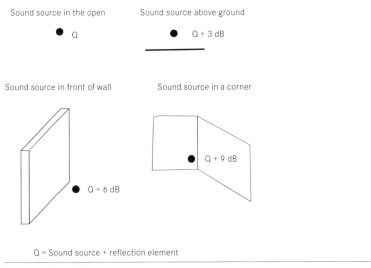

Sound source in the open

● Q

Sound source above ground

● Q + 3 dB

Sound source in front of wall

● Q + 6 dB

Sound source in a corner

● Q + 9 dB

Q = Sound source + reflection element

Fig. 9: Location of the source of noise

Sound-screening objects

The propagation of sound can be significantly affected by sound-screening objects such as <u>noise-attenuating banks or walls</u>. In this case, the sound energy is partially reflected and partially absorbed by the surface of the object. The amount of sound absorbed depends on the properties of the surface. In the case of noise protection walls with a concrete surface, the largest part is reflected. Owing to what is called the diffraction effect, part of the sound energy bypasses the noise protection wall, a phenomenon that occurs particularly because of the long wavelength, especially at low frequencies. In practice, this means that the effect of a noise protection wall or a noise protection bank is limited. > Fig. 10

When designing a sound-screening object, it is important for the object to interrupt the sightline between the source of the noise and the place of immission. The larger the distance between the source of the sound and the place of immission, the greater the sound-reducing effect. > Fig. 11

In order to achieve adequate sound screening, the respective object must be high enough and afford sufficient sound attenuation. As a rule of thumb, this should be at least 25 dB.

○ **Note**: Owing to the diffraction effect, which means that part of the sound energy always bypasses the noise protection wall, the effect is limited to max. 25 dB.

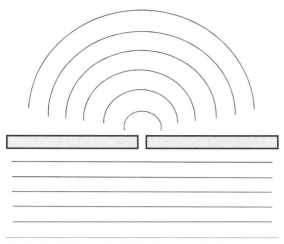

Fig. 10: Illustration of sound diffraction at a small opening

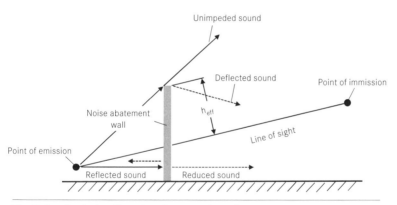

Fig. 11: Sound-reducing effect of a noise protection wall

For example, when a noise protection wall with a hard surface (e.g., concrete or glass) is built to protect a building, it is possible that this results in unwanted reflections that have a negative acoustic effect on the opposite side. These reflections can be reduced by a sound-absorbing surface on the noise protection wall. In this case, the sound energy is converted to heat through friction at the sound-absorbing surface.

Sound reflections and sound shadows at building facades

As well as noise protection walls or banks, it is also possible for buildings to function as sound-screening objects. Here, too, it is important to take into account any reflections that may affect buildings on the opposite side.

Modern buildings with their smooth, acoustically hard facades of render, fair-faced concrete, brick, or glass increase the sound level due to reflections. This effect can be mitigated with the help of sound-absorbing or sound-scattering facades; this requires the facades to be somewhat more porous and therefore frequently counteracts the original function of the facade, which is to protect the loadbearing building structure from the effects of the weather. > Fig. 12

Vegetation-based attenuation

When calculating the sound level across a wooded area, a certain amount of scattering and screening caused by the tree trunks, branches, and leaves has to be taken into account as this reduces the sound level. However, the resulting vegetation-based attenuation only results in a small reduction in the sound pressure level.

Ground-based attenuation

In the case of sound propagating close to the ground, the sound pressure level is reduced by ground-based attenuation (ground effect). This effect reduces the higher frequencies more strongly than the lower frequencies, which means that, at a greater distance, lower frequencies can be heard in the form of very low-pitched sound.

Meteorological impacts

In addition to the geometric conditions impacting sound propagation, there are other effects that can dampen the sound level. Owing to certain specific characteristics of air, such as temperature, relative humidity, and the suspension of dirt particles, sound may be absorbed in the air. In this case, the sound energy is converted to heat through friction of the air particles. Air-based attenuation affects higher frequencies more than lower frequencies.

The farther you are away from the source of the sound, the more dominant are the lower frequencies and the sound is heard more as a deep hum.

When assessing the sound level across greater distances, it is particularly important to take into account meteorological influences such as wind. If wind and sound have the same direction, the propagation of the sound is reinforced. By contrast, in the counter-wind direction the propagation of sound is reduced.

■ **Tip**: It is possible to absorb or scatter sound with the help of facade greening. Another useful aid is to provide facades with a surface structure, for example by providing projections and recesses, balconies, or tilted facade elements.

● **Example**: This effect has been especially noticed with large sporting events in the open in which the public and the commentator can be heard more or less clearly from a greater distance, depending on the direction of the wind.

Fig. 12: Sound-absorbing facades with a surface structure

Sound propagation is also affected by the <u>temperature of the air</u>. When the air temperature rises above the sound source, the sound is diffracted downwards. This so-called <u>inversion effect</u> leads to greater transmission distances. However, when the ground is heated by solar irradiation, the speed of sound propagation is reduced and the sound is diffracted upwards. At a certain distance from the source of the sound, this creates areas with a sound shadow. > Fig. 13

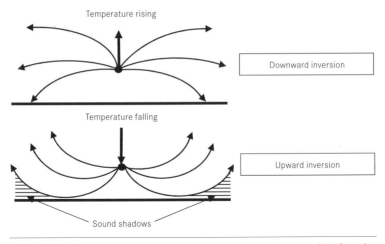

Fig. 13: Inversion resulting from the temperature rising (top); inversion resulting from the temperature falling (bottom)

When considering acoustic effects in rooms, for example in the assessment of room acoustics or of sound levels within industrial buildings, other physical parameters have to be taken into account. Whereas in the open the sound pressure level reduces with increasing distance, the pressure level of sound propagating in rooms, from a certain distance from the source of the sound, is independent of one's position in the room owing to reflections from the walls and floors, etc. > Chapter Room acoustics

PERCEPTION OF SOUND

The underlying purpose of assessing sound levels is to find out how they affect the surroundings and people exposed to the sounds. Below, we discuss the mechanism of how sounds are perceived by humans, how noise affects people, and what special aspects need to be taken into consideration.

Sound pressure travels via the ear conch and the ear canal to the eardrum and causes it to vibrate. The eardrum conducts the sound energy via the middle ear to the inner ear (cochlea). Here, another membrane excites the hair cells, which transmit nervous signals (i.e., electrical signals) to the brain. > Fig. 14

The human ear perceives sounds in the frequency range of 16 Hz to 20,000 Hz; sounds below 16 Hz are perceived as some sort of rumble (infrasound). With increasing age, perception of the upper frequency

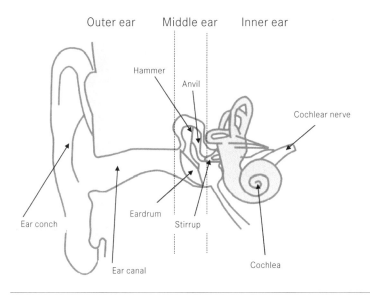

Outer ear   Middle ear   Inner ear

Hammer

Anvil

Cochlear nerve

Ear conch

Eardrum

Stirrup

Ear canal

Cochlea

Fig. 14: Diagram of the human ear

range is reduced owing to wear of the hair cells. The hair cells can also suffer permanent damage due to continuous exposure to noise or due to exposure to very high sound level peaks. Loss of hearing due to exposure to noise first affects the higher frequencies (approx. 4,000 Hz), a fact that particularly impedes verbal communication in rooms with higher background noise levels (e.g., public houses, open-plan offices). Damage to the hair cells is not reversible; furthermore, hair cells do not regrow.

Within the range of perception stated above, the sensitivity of the human ear heavily depends on frequency. The ear is significantly more sensitive to medium and higher frequencies than to low and very high frequencies. Sound pressure levels with equal loudness contours, but different frequencies are not perceived as being equally loud. > Fig. 15

In addition to sound pressure and sound pressure level, the term "loudness" is used for the purpose of comparing the subjective perception of different sound levels by the ear. This is based on the subjective comparison of a tone with a reference tone of 1,000 Hz. This means that, at 1,000 Hz, the loudness scale corresponds exactly to the decibel scale. In order to determine the loudness, the signal is compared

Frequency dependency of the human ear

Loudness

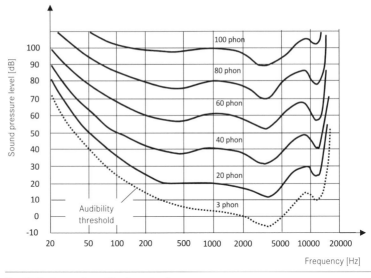

Fig. 15: Contours of equal loudness levels

to the reference tone at 1,000 Hz. The unit of measure of loudness is
○ phon.

In view of the fact that determining loudness is relatively complex
and hence expensive, level values that take into account the sensitivity
of the human ear have been defined for measuring sound pressure levels. These are referred to as the frequency weighting curves A to C. The
A-weighting curve is used for low loudness, the B-weighting curve for medium loudness, and the C-weighting curve for high loudness. Because the
A-weighting curve is closest to human perception, it is usually used nowadays when measuring sound levels.

As can be seen in Fig. 16, the A-weighting curve reduces the sound
level at the low and high frequencies.

○ **Note**: In view of the fact that loudness is a purely
subjective variable, it can't be measured. What is
measured is the sound pressure, or rather the sound
pressure level. For a measured sound pressure level
of 60 dB, the loudness referenced against a frequency
of 100 Hz is approx. 50 phon, and referenced against
a frequency of 2,000 Hz is approx. 61 phon.

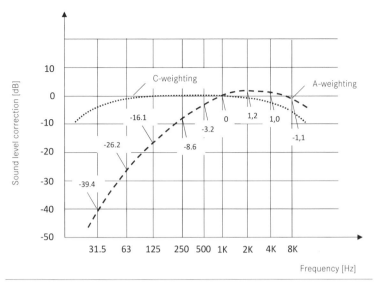

Fig. 16: A- and C-weighting curves

The term "noise" refers to sound that is perceived as disagreeable, polluting, and unwelcome, i.e., as <u>undesirable sound</u>. Which sound events this applies to depends on the subjective perception of the respective person. The acceptance of a certain type of noise often increases when the perceiving person benefits from the source of the noise. For example, if a person frequently travels by rail, this person will have greater acceptance of the noise produced by trains because the proximity of the railway is a clear benefit.

In contrast to the time before industrialization, people today are exposed to numerous sources of noise that may be of long duration and strong intensity, for example, road and rail traffic, aviation, industrial and commercial activities, construction, leisure activities (open-air concerts), and activities in the neighbourhood (lawnmowers, leaf vacuums, etc.).

Noise can have a long-term detrimental effect on the health of humans. High levels of sustained noise pollution and exposure to high sound pressure levels (e.g., from industry and commerce, discos, etc.) can lead to impaired hearing or to being hard of hearing if hearing protection is inadequate.

The effect of exposure to lower noise levels can also result in a negative impact on health. This may take the form of sleep disorders, lack of concentration, heart palpitations (high blood pressure), reduced efficiency, and poor communication. > Table 3

Table 3: Effect of noise on humans

Examples of noise	Sound pressure level [dB(A)]	Effect of noise
Airplane at a distance of 7 m	130	Pain threshold
Discotheque	110	
Compressed air hammer	100	Unbearable
Construction vehicles at a distance of 1 m	95	
Circular saw, motorbike	90	
	85	May cause damage to
Passenger car at a distance of 1 m	80	hearing
Main road, daytime	75	
Air traffic	70	
Rail traffic, lawnmower	65	The risk of cardiovascu-
Main road, nighttime	60	lar disease increases
	55	Loud
Normal conversation	50	
Ticking of an alarm clock	30	
Rustling of leaves	25	Soft
Hourglass	20	
Dripping water faucet	10	
	5	Quiet
	0	Auditory threshold

Of particular importance are sleep disorders because during the night, the human body needs to recover from the day's stresses.

Sound immission protection

Sound immission protection deals with the noise impacting on a building from its surroundings. Noise arising from the surroundings is considered to be the noise created by people, including the noise from road, rail, and air traffic and noise emitted from commercial or industrial facilities. The objective is to protect people from excessive noise pollution by devising specific planning or design measures at the source of the noise or at the property under consideration.

PROTECTION OBJECTIVES

In order to ensure that residential and work areas are sufficiently quiet, the internal rooms of a building, as well as spaces in the open such as balconies, terraces, playgrounds, etc., need to be protected from excessive noise pollution. In addition, users should be able to ventilate residential and work areas naturally by opening windows without having to suffer excessive noise. If the national limits or guide values are not complied with, additional noise protection measures must be put in place. A distinction is made between measures at the source (active sound protection measures) and measures at the recipient (passive sound protection measures).

Grades of noise

■

EMISSION – IMMISSION

<u>Sound emission</u> refers to the sound emitted from a sound source, such as a commercial facility. <u>Sound immission</u> refers to sound that impacts on people or a building. A further distinction is made between sound immissions that impact a building via airborne sound (primary sound) and those that impact on the structure via the vibrations of physical bodies (secondary sound). In secondary sound, the building components in the ground (foundations, cellar walls, etc.) are excited and transmit the excitation energy to the building structure. Within the building, this energy is emitted via the building structure (e.g., walls and floors) to the internal rooms as airborne sound. > Fig. 17

■ **Tip:** In view of the fact that active noise protection measures at the source of the noise are usually more effective than passive noise protection measures at the place of immission, these should preferably be chosen for sound immission protection.

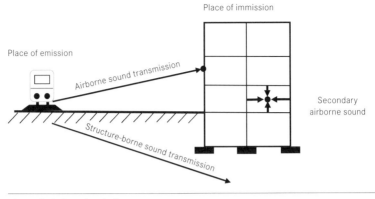

Place of immission

Place of emission

Airborne sound transmission

Structure-borne sound transmission

Secondary
airborne sound

Fig. 17: Emission – immission

ASSESSMENT OF SOUND IMMISSIONS

Assessment level   For the purpose of assessing noise immissions, the A-weighting sound pressure level is determined at the respective building. This can be done by calculation or by measurement. In view of the fact that the loudness of noises varies (e.g., trains passing), the average value of the sound pressure level over time is used for assessing the sound immissions. In addition, it is necessary to add an amount as a loading to the sound pressure level determined, depending on tonality and impulsiveness. Examples of this are the noises from building services equipment and delivery processes at commercial premises (shops, hotels, logistics companies, etc.). The sum of the sound pressure level determined and the adjustments based on tonality and impulsiveness result in the assessment level, which is then compared with the applicable national limits and guide values.

Guide values of   In view of the fact that the noise from traffic, commercial premises,
sound immissions   or leisure activities is not always perceived as equally polluting, in spite of identical average levels, different immission guide values apply depending on the type of noise pollution. In addition, these guide values also depend on the local position of the respective building. For example, if the building is located in a mixed-use area with both commercial and residential properties, the user expectation and tolerance of higher sound pressure levels are greater than in areas classed as purely residential.

Determining sound   The measurement of noises is carried out with sound level meters.
immissions   > Fig. 18 When this is done at the place of immission, it usually serves to check that the immission guide values are complied with. In certain cases, measurements at the place of immission do not give the required results because a number of different sources of noise can't be unequivocally

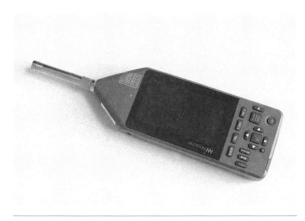

Fig. 18: Sound level meter

allocated. This may be the case, for example, where noises from industrial and commercial premises are superposed. In these cases, it is necessary to take measurements at the place of emission in order to determine the sound pressure level or sound power level. Using the values from these measurements, it is then possible to calculate the sound pressure level at the place of immission. This calculation needs to take screening objects, sound-reflecting building components, and possibly meteorological factors into account.

When designing new buildings or structures, and also for the purpose of carrying out conversions to buildings and parts of structures, it is common to carry out a sound immission calculation. As a rule, this is done using 3D calculation programs, with which it is possible, with adequate accuracy, to model the noise emissions and the surroundings, including any sound-screening objects and sound-reflecting building components. The resulting values represent a prognosis, which can be used to determine any conflicting situations with respect to noise at an early design stage.

LEGAL BACKGROUND

As a rule, legislation is in place that governs the control of immissions. For example, in Germany the Federal Immission Control Act (BImSchG) provides the legal basis for sound immission protection. Immission control legislation is intended to protect humans, animals, and plants from hazardous environmental effects. It is often necessary to clarify, when building permission is granted or even beforehand, what emissions into the environment are to be expected from a permanent structure (commercial/industrial premises, services installations, leisure

Immission control legislation

27

facilities, etc.) or from a movable plant (machines and equipment that are not part of public transport), and whether the applicable national regulations are complied with. The granting of building permission also takes into account technically feasible conditions, as well as the proportional-
■ ity of the financial burden.

In residential buildings, the objective of sound immission protection is to create healthy living conditions. This can be achieved with noise-reducing measures at the source of the sound, by appropriate orientation of the building and a favourable plan layout design, as well as planning-based sound protection measures.

NOISE-REDUCING MEASURES

Emission-reducing measures are most effective at the source of the noise, for example, at the vehicles themselves. For road traffic vehicles, this can be achieved, for example, by encapsulating the engine appropriately or by reducing the rolling noise of the tires. Noise-reducing measures are particularly effective when applied to heavy goods vehicles. When dealing with rail-based traffic, noise can be reduced, for example, by using quieter braking material (whisper brakes) or tire absorbers.

It may also be possible to reduce noise by choosing suitable surface finishes on roads or rail tracks. For example, roads finished with paviours create more noise than those finished with asphalt. Furthermore, it is now becoming popular to use open-pored, sound-absorbing asphalt finishes, so-called "whisper asphalt," which produce their greatest effect
○ at speeds from 60 km/h.

Additional noise-reducing measures at the source may consist of a reduction in the traffic volume and travel speed, and sound-screening solid building components such as noise protection walls, noise protection banks, and the placement of buildings that have a noise-screening effect on otherwise exposed buildings located behind them. > Fig. 19

■ **Tip:** The design of structures is subject to the <u>precautionary and polluter pays principle</u>, which means that the design has to ensure, from the very beginning, that no hazards are created for the environment in the future. As a rule, any required measures have to be paid for by the polluter.

○ **Note**: When newly laid, whisper asphalt can achieve a reduction in noise level of up to 5 dB(A). However, it is important to note that these finishes are less durable than common asphalt finishes and that, over time, the pores become clogged, which diminishes the noise-reducing effect.

● **Example**: Halving the traffic volume achieves a 3 dB reduction in the emission level; reducing the maximum speed from 50 km/h to 30 km/h achieves an approx. 2 to 3 dB reduction in the emission level.

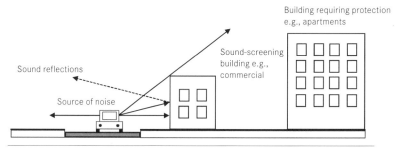

Fig. 19: Sound-screening measures

BUILDING ORIENTATION AND FLOOR PLAN DESIGN

In view of today's demand for housing, particularly in the inner cities, developments in areas exposed to high levels of pollution from road and rail traffic, as well as from commercial premises, are almost inevitable. For developments in areas subject to noise pollution, it is possible to mitigate noise emissions with an appropriate building orientation and building shape, as well as a favourable plan layout design. The objective here is to arrange rooms in need of protection, such as bedrooms and living rooms, on the side of the building that faces away from the source of noise.

Where the source of noise, such as road or rail traffic, is only on one side of the building, this can be achieved by adopting a floor plan design in which bathrooms, corridors, and stairwells, i.e., rooms that are less sensitive to noise, are placed on the side facing the source of the noise and all or some of the noise-sensitive rooms are placed on the side facing away from the source of the noise. It is also possible to provide open-plan rooms that have a facade on both sides, facing the source of the noise and facing away from it. This at least gives the user the option to ventilate the room by opening the window on the quiet side. > Fig. 20

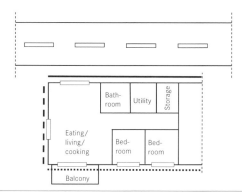

Fig. 20: Rooms in need of protection face away from the source of noise

In order to be able to protect the sides of the building that face away from the noise from sound immission from the side, <u>semi-open forms of building</u> can be helpful. In this type of building, it is possible to place noise-sensitive rooms around a quiet inner courtyard, which has the added advantage of providing recreational space for everyone. Regarding the sides of the building that face away from the source of noise, it is important to take into account any sound-increasing reflections from other structures to the side or behind the building. > Fig. 21

Another option that is particularly suitable in the case of dispersed sources of noise is to place a continuous row of buildings along the edge of a site. In this type of development, the apartments are placed around an inner courtyard, and the plan layouts are designed such that noise-sensitive rooms face this inner courtyard. However, this type of development occupies a relatively large proportion of the site surface because the inner courtyard has to be sufficiently large to afford adequate daylight. In this type of design, it is important to ensure that there are no other noise-polluting technical installations in the inner courtyard, such as heat pumps, ventilation plant. > Fig. 22

In some cases, it is not possible or not desirable from a conceptual point of view to arrange noise-sensitive rooms facing away from the source of noise. This can be the case where buildings are built on sloping terrain. In these cases, it is nevertheless possible to achieve sufficient noise protection by creating terraces. In addition, the noise-attenuating effect can be significantly increased by adding solid, closed parapets. > Fig. 23

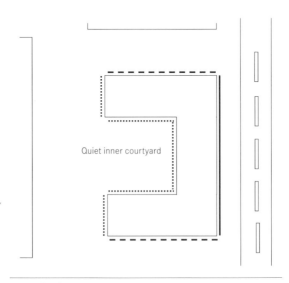

Quiet inner courtyard

Fig. 21: Semi-open building shape

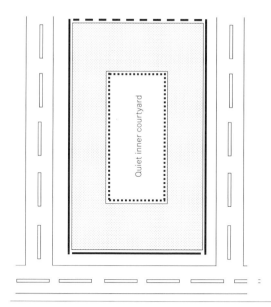

Fig. 22: Building around an inner courtyard

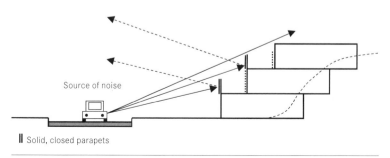

Fig. 23: Buildings in terraced formation

DESIGN-BASED NOISE PROTECTION MEASURES

In addition to devising a suitable plan layout, there are other design measures that can be used to achieve noise attenuation. An example is to place oriels or small bays on the side facades of the building. These have the advantage of placing the ventilating window on the side of the bay facing away from the noise. In order to achieve adequate noise attenuation, the window must be far enough away from the corner of the bay. > Fig. 24

In the design of plan layouts, it is often not possible to place all noise-sensitive rooms away from the source of noise. This can be addressed by placing loggias in front of the room to be protected, thereby creating quieter outside spaces. These can be built with partially open glazing and, if appropriate, with sound-absorbing ceiling panels. Where it is possible to open the glazed portion, the user benefits from a direct connection to the outside. It is important that the glazing has adequate sound insulation. > Figs. 25 and 26

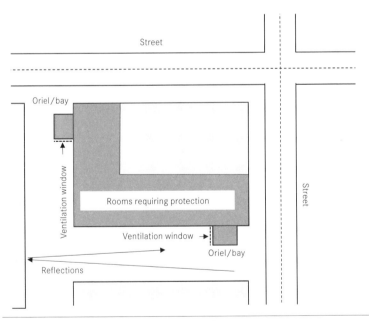

Fig. 24: Placement of oriels/bays as a noise protection measure

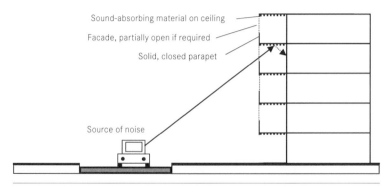

Sound-absorbing material on ceiling

Facade, partially open if required

Solid, closed parapet

Source of noise

Fig. 25: Loggias as a noise protection measure

Fig. 26: Loggias with partially openable glazing

Building acoustics

Whereas in sound immission protection the subject of investigation is the sound impacting a building, building acoustics aims to protect people inside the building from excessive sound transmission from outside the unit. This involves designing partition elements such as external walls, roofs, windows, and walls and floors between apartments with adequate sound insulation. In addition, noise generated by services installations (elevators, water installations, ventilation aggregates, etc.) must be minimized. The development of building components and sound-reducing measures requires extensive knowledge of the sound-insulating properties of materials and of component design. For this reason, the most important task in building acoustics is to determine the effectiveness of sound insulation by measurement and calculation. Below, we describe the key fundamentals and provide notes on design.

AIRBORNE SOUND – IMPACT SOUND

In building acoustics, a distinction is made between airborne sound and impact sound; impact sound refers to a special form of structure-borne sound.

Airborne sound

Airborne sound refers to the sound that propagates via the vibration of particles in air. The sound propagated in this way impacts on the building component and is then dispersed in weakened form from the other side. In addition to this direct sound transmission, the separating building component also transmits the sound via flanking components such as floors, ceilings, and lateral walls. > Fig. 27

Impact sound

Impact sound refers to the direct mechanical excitation of a separate building component through impact (footfall) on a floor, staircase, or stair landing. Such impact will cause direct flexural vibration to the building component, which will lead to sound being dispersed from the component into the adjacent room. When dealing with floors, staircases, etc., we usually talk about impact sound. The activity of exciting a building component, for example, through drilling, knocking, or hammering, is generally referred to as structure-borne sound excitation.

Where a building component is excited by impact, the resulting sound is transmitted via transmission pathways to the room directly underneath, as well as in horizontal and diagonal directions, and to the rooms above. > Fig. 28

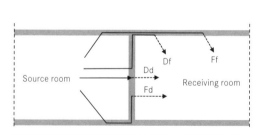
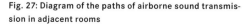

Df
Dd
Fd
Ff

Source room
Receiving room

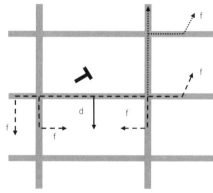

f
d
f
f
f
f

Fig. 27: Diagram of the paths of airborne sound transmission in adjacent rooms

Fig. 28: Transmission pathways of impact sound in
adjacent rooms

KEY BUILDING ACOUSTICS VARIABLES

When considering the <u>airborne sound insulation</u> of a separating
building component, the objective is to ensure that as little sound energy as possible is transmitted into the adjacent rooms. For example, a
loudspeaker placed in a room – the source room – transmits the sound
via the directly separating building component, as well as via secondary
pathways in the flanking building components (adjacent walls, ceilings,
etc.) or via openings and holes for services. The sound level is measured
in the receiving room. > Fig. 27 Put simply, the airborne sound insulation
of a separating building component is the difference between the sound
level in the source room and that in the receiving room. The greater the
sound level difference, the better the sound insulation of the building
component.

Airborne sound
insulation, airborne
sound reduction index

○

○ **Note**: The quality of sound insulation of a separating
component is often determined in a test laboratory
as part of research work or following the commission
from a product manufacturer. In this case, the <u>airborne
sound reduction indices</u> are measured on the basis of
ideal installation conditions. When the same component is tested for its sound insulation after installation
in the building, the airborne sound reduction index is
normally not as good owing to the actual installation
conditions. It is important that this matter is taken into
account when designing the sound insulation of separating components.

Once the airborne sound reduction index has been determined, taking into account secondary pathways of sound transmission, it must be compared with the respective national standards.

Sound pressure
level difference

The sound reduction index described above is used to describe the sound insulation quality of the component. However, when assessing the reduction of the noise transmitted through the separating component from one room to an adjacent room, it is preferable to investigate the <u>sound pressure level difference</u>. This depends not only on the sound insulation quality of the separating component but also on the configuration of flanking components and the respective properties of the room.

For example, if a room has strong reverberations, the sound pressure level is perceived to be higher compared to a room with fewer reverberations due to sound-absorbing materials. The sound pressure level difference is used to describe the subjective perception of noise reduction.

Impact sound
insulation

To determine the impact sound insulation of a separating component (e.g., a floor slab), the sound level in the source room is determined in parallel to the structure-borne sound excitation of the component. In this case, the structure-borne sound is transmitted directly via the separating component and the flanking components.

Once the impact sound insulation has been determined, taking into account secondary pathways, it must be compared with the respective national standards.

○ **Note**: For the purpose of determining the impact sound insulation of a floor slab, the level in the receiving room is measured rather than the difference in sound levels. This means the lower the measured sound level, the better the sound insulation.

INFLUENCE OF SECONDARY PATHWAY TRANSMISSION

Airborne sound is not only transmitted via the separating building component but also via <u>secondary pathways</u>. For airborne sound insulation, the building components in direct contact with the separating building component are relevant, for example, flanking walls, floors, and ceilings, as well as openings or unintended apertures in the separating component itself (cracks or gaps, ventilation openings, pipe penetrations, etc.). Very often, these secondary pathways have a significant impact on the resulting sound insulation of the separating building component. Important details are not only the dimensions and the design of the flanking component but also how the respective joints are designed and executed. Lightweight flanking components, such as floating screeds and suspended ceilings that continue above or beneath a separating wall without interruption, significantly reduce the sound insulation of the separating component. If, by contrast, the screed or the suspended ceiling is interrupted in the area of the separating building component, it is possible to achieve significant improvement with these components. > Fig. 29

Secondary airborne sound transmission pathways

Very often it is not possible to interrupt a flanking building component in the area of the separating wall, for example, for structural reasons. In order to achieve adequate sound insulation of the separating building component all the same, the flanking component must either have enough mass or be fitted with a second skin. In this case, the second skin functions as a protective shield that ensures that the flanking building component is excited as little as possible by the sound energy.

Impact sound is created when a solid component, such as a separating building component, is directly excited (e.g., walking across a floor slab). In the case of stair runs, and also balconies, impact sound is primarily transmitted vertically but also in a horizontal and/or diagonal direction. Depending on the direction of transmission, correction values can be applied to the calculation of the impact sound. For example, when assessing the impact sound insulation between a balcony and a habitable

Impact sound transmission pathways

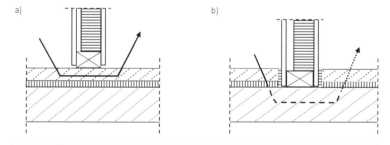

Fig. 29: a) Screed, continuous (unfavourable) b) Screed, interrupted (favourable)

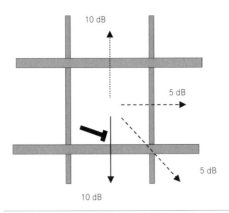

Fig. 30: Correction values for different transmission directions

space diagonally beneath, it is possible to apply a reduction of approx. 5 dB to the impact sound transmission value. > Fig. 30

SINGLE-SKIN BUILDING COMPONENTS

In building acoustics, a distinction is made between single-skin and double-skin building components. In single-skin elements, it is the mass per square area of the separating building component that provides airborne sound insulation. Typical single-skin components are, for example, masonry walls or reinforced concrete walls. When these are finished with a layer of plaster, they are nevertheless referred to as single-skin components.

Berger's mass law   According to <u>Berger's mass law</u>, the airborne sound insulation of single-skin building components increases proportionally to the mass per square area. This mass is calculated by multiplying the bulk density δ of the material by the thickness d of the building component. If the component has several layers, for example, a layer of plaster, these are included in the calculation of the mass per square area, even though these additional layers do not usually add significantly to the sound insulation of the separating component. Having said that, the layer of plaster on a masonry wall has an extra sealing function as it helps to seal off any air gaps in the separating wall. The following diagram (> Fig. 31) can be used to determine the airborne sound insulation of a single-skin component
● consisting of material with a certain mass per square area.

> ● **Example**: Masonry d = 15 cm, bulk density
> δ = 1,900 kg/m² → m' = 285 kg/m²; the Gösele
> curve in Fig. 32 indicates an airborne sound
> insulation value R_w of ≈ 48 dB

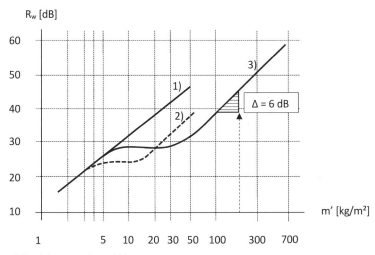

1) Steel sheet up to 2 mm thick
2) Wood and wood-based materials
3) Gypsum materials; concrete, masonry

Fig. 31: Gösele curve airborne sound insulation in relation to material and mass

Fig. 31 shows in the curves for gypsum material, concrete, and masonry, as well as for wood-based materials, that there are areas in which the sound insulation does not increase in spite of an increase in the mass per square area. The reason for this is that the flexural rigidity of the construction increases with increasing thickness of the wall or panel/board.

In addition, Berger's mass law states that doubling the frequency or the mass per square area results in an improvement in the airborne sound insulation of 6 dB.

○

○ **Note**: This improvement of 6 dB is only a theoretical notion because the mass law presumes that the sound vertically impacts the separating building component and that there is an ideal diffuse sound field. In practice, sound impacts the component not only vertically but also diagonally.

In addition to the mass law described above, the so-called <u>critical coincidence frequency</u> is important for determining the airborne sound insulation of the separating building component. For example, when the sound generated by a person speaking impacts diagonally on a separating wall, flexural vibration results in the wall. The sound impacting on the separating building component propagates along the wall as airborne sound. The sound transmitted by a single-skin component is particularly loud when the wavelength of the airborne sound λ_L is identical to the flexural wave λ_E of the building component. > Fig. 32

In order to ensure that the effectiveness of the airborne sound insulation is not compromised too much by the critical coincidence frequency, the critical frequency range of the component should be chosen to be
○ outside the range that is critical from the building acoustics point of view.

In practice, one usually limits calculations to the range between 160 Hz and 2,000 Hz, as this is the critical range that is also the relevant frequency range in building acoustics. Building components with a critical coincidence frequency of less than 160 Hz are considered sufficiently flexurally rigid, and components over 2,000 Hz sufficiently flexurally soft. Table 4 lists a few examples of building components that may be used in practice.

As a general principle, flexurally rigid components such as masonry walls should be as flexurally rigid as possible, whereas components such
○■ as the linings of drywall partitions are flexurally soft.

○ **Note**: The critical coincidence frequency varies with the material's bulk density ρ, the thickness of the building component d, and the modulus of elasticity E_{dyn} and can be calculated as follows:

$$f_g \cong \frac{60}{d \times \sqrt{\frac{\rho}{E_{dyn}}}} \quad [\text{Hz}]$$

whereby:
d = thickness of building component in m
ρ = bulk density of material in kg/m³
E_{dyn} = dynamic modulus of elasticity of material in MN/m²

○ **Note**: Solid walls with a mass per square area of ≤ 200 kg/m² need special consideration because the coincidence frequency is exactly in the range that is relevant for building acoustics. In particular, this applies to gypsum, aerated concrete, and pumice concrete walls with thicknesses of between 6 and 12 cm.

■ **Tip**: When designing drywall partitions, the thickness of the boards should be limited to max. 18 mm owing to the critical coincidence frequency. Where greater mass per square area is required, it is preferable to apply two or three layers.

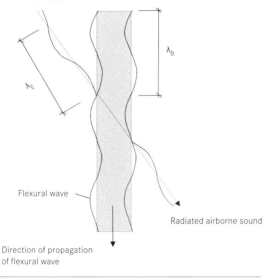

Incident airborne sound

λ_B

λ_E

Flexural wave

Radiated airborne sound

Direction of propagation
of flexural wave

Fig. 32: Excitation and dispersal of flexural waves

Table 4: Examples of building components with their critical coincidence frequencies

Building component	Thickness d [cm]	Critical coincidence frequency f_g [Hz]
Brick masonry	11.5	220
Concrete wall	20	85
Gypsum board	1.25	2,500
Chipboard	2	1,300

DOUBLE-SKIN BUILDING COMPONENTS

Double-skin building components are components consisting of two independent skins. The gap between the two skins is left as an air gap or filled with soft, springy insulation material in order to achieve the best possible separation. In acoustics, this construction is referred to as a mass-spring-mass system; the two skins of the wall are considered the mass elements and the air or mineral insulation between the skins is referred to as the spring. With double-skin elements, it is possible to achieve significantly higher sound reduction indices compared to single-skin building components. In practice and depending on the design, the skins are connected to each other where they meet at the adjoining building components and, in the case of drywall construction (metal or

timber stud partitions), the skins are also connected where they are attached to the studs. These connections must be taken into account when
● designing double-skin structures. > Fig. 33

Resonance frequency   When designing a double-skin structure, it is important to note that, at a certain frequency (e.g., when excited by speech), the two skins always resonate. At this particular frequency, the two skins of the wall vibrate in a very unfavourable manner, which leads to a significant reduc-
○● tion in the sound insulation.

a = Skin 1 of wall (mass 1),
     e.g., brickwork
b = Mineral insulation
     (spring)
c = Skin 2 of wall (mass 2),
     e.g., brickwork

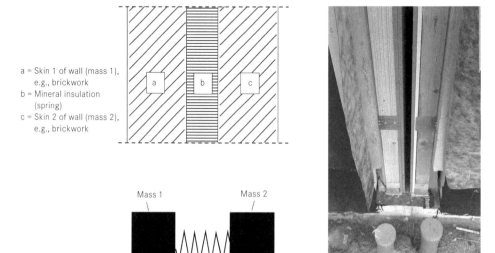

Fig. 33: Double-skin wall construction with mass-spring-mass system. Photo: Double-stud wall in timber frame construction

● **Example**: Typical double-skin structures are, for example, external or separating cavity walls, floating screed, and plasterboard stud partitions.

● **Example**: A masonry cavity wall with d = 17.5 cm and m' = 330 kg/m² for each skin, with mineral insulation with a dynamic flexural rigidity of s' = 10 MN/m³ between the skins, results in a resonance frequency f_0 of 40 Hz.

○ **Note**: Essentially, the resonance frequency depends on the mass per square area of the skins and the flexural rigidity of the spring (the intermediate layer) and can be calculated as follows:

$$f_0 = 160 \times \sqrt{s' \times \left(\tfrac{1}{m'_1} + \tfrac{1}{m'_2}\right)} \quad [Hz]$$

whereby:
s = dynamic flexural rigidity of insulating layer in MN/m³
m' = mass per square area of the respective skin of the wall in kg/m²

In order to achieve adequate sound insulation with double-skin structures, appropriate construction details should be used to ensure that the resonance frequency – as a minimum – is below the frequency range relevant to building acoustics. This can be achieved by increasing the mass of the respective component skins and by choosing an intermediate layer, the flexural spring rigidity of which is as low as possible. A greater distance between the skins of the wall also has a positive effect on the sound insulation. Fig. 34 shows curves for the airborne sound insulation of a double-skin building component. In Section 1, the sound insulation of the double-skin structure is identical to that of a single-skin structure. In Section 2, the sound insulation of the cavity wall dramatically worsens owing to the resonance frequency, resulting in a poorer sound reduction index compared to a single-skin wall of identical mass. In Section 3, the sound reduction index of the cavity wall is significantly greater than that of a single-skin wall of equal mass.　　　　　　　　○

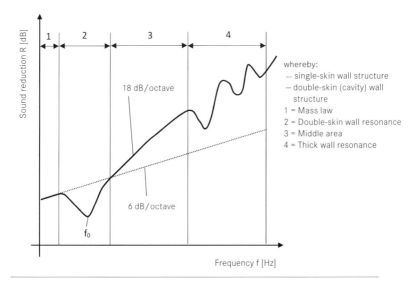

Fig. 34: Comparison of sound reduction curves of double-skin and single-skin structures

○ **Note**: Resonance frequencies of between 100 Hz and 4,000 Hz are critical. The basic principle is the lower the resonance frequency f_0, the better the sound reduction because the lower frequency sounds are better attenuated.

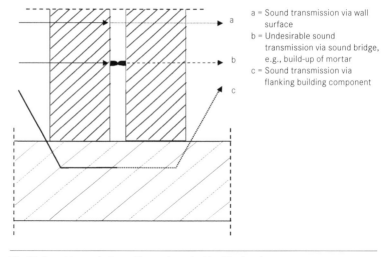

a = Sound transmission via wall surface

b = Undesirable sound transmission via sound bridge, e.g., build-up of mortar

c = Sound transmission via flanking building component

Fig. 35: Sound transmission pathways for a double-skin structure

Sound bridges

Ideally, the sound is only transmitted via the double-skin wall and, normally, via the unavoidable connection around the edges, for example, along the floor slab and the ceiling. > Fig. 35 If it is not possible to neatly separate any flanking building components around the edges, these components must have sufficient mass. Alternatively, it is possible to reduce the amount of sound transmitted by using additional skins at the flanks

■ or by disconnecting the edges using special insulation strips.

Plasterboard walls

Good sound reduction indices can't only be achieved with double-skin wall structures consisting of flexurally rigid masonry walls as described above but also with drywall construction using flexurally soft skins, for example, plasterboard. These must not be too thick in order to

■ **Tip:** It is imperative to avoid sound bridges such as those caused by mortar droppings in the cavity between the brick skins that can build up and bridge the gap entirely. For this reason, it is recommended to fill the gap with soft, springy mineral insulation, in particular in the gap between the two skins of a cavity wall. Furthermore, this mineral insulation adds to the sound reduction across the cavity.

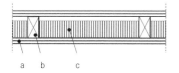 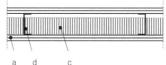

a = Plasterboard or
    gypsum fibreboard
b = Wooden studs
c = Mineral insulation
d = Metal studs (C-profile)

Fig. 36: Double-skin wall construction using flexurally soft skins

ensure that the coincidence frequency of the boards/panels does not fall into the range that is relevant for building acoustics. Where greater mass of the individual layers is required, additional layers should be added rather than opting for thicker boards. This will only insignificantly reduce the critical coincidence frequency. > Fig. 36

Owing to the flexural softness of the two skins, it is necessary to insert metal or timber studs. However, by connecting the two skins, the improved sound reduction of the two-skin component to above the resonance frequency is significantly lessened. Connecting the two skins via the studs has the effect of a sound bridge; this must be countered as much as possible by using elastic connectors or by inserting a flexurally soft insulation layer. Owing to their elastic properties, wall studs consisting of thin metal sheeting (e.g., C-profile) have proven to be useful. Where it is intended to completely decouple the two skins of the wall, it is possible to use double studs or separate freestanding skins.

The insulation in the cavity between the skins has a major impact on the resonance frequency and hence the sound reduction of the building component. In the area of the studs, the sound reduction is relatively poor; the cavity between the studs should be filled with open-pored sound-absorbing material. The sound is reduced by the fibres in the different layers rubbing against each other, thereby converting the sound energy into heat. This reduces resonance effects and reflections in the cavity. Examples of possible insulation material are mineral-fibre and wood-fibre insulation and insulation materials consisting of sheep's wool or cotton. Plastic insulation material with closed pores, such as polystyrene board, polyurethane foam board, etc., should be avoided.   ○

○ **Note**: The insulation material used should have suitable resistance, so-called flow resistivity. This should be between 5 kPa s/m and 50 kPa s/m. We will discuss flow resistivity in greater detail in the Room acoustics chapter.

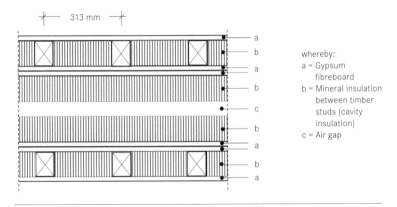

Fig. 37: Double-skin timber frame wall with reduced spacing between studs

whereby:
a = Gypsum
fibreboard
b = Mineral insulation
between timber
studs (cavity
insulation)
c = Air gap

In drywall construction, the depth of the studs has a relatively small influence on the overall sound reduction of the separating building component. However, changing the stud grid will cause changes to the sound reduction in the low and medium frequency ranges. This property is made use of, for example, in timber party walls between buildings. By reducing the distance between studs from 625 mm to about 313 mm, a sound reduction in the low frequency range is significantly improved. > Fig. 37

Optimizing single-skin building components Where it is necessary to <u>optimize the airborne sound insulation</u> of solid single-skin walls, for example, masonry or reinforced concrete walls, it is recommended to use an additional flexurally soft skin. In this case, it is important to choose the correct resonance frequency and to take the coincidence effect into account. If possible, the coincidence frequency of the solid wall should be modified towards the low frequencies, i.e., the wall should be as flexurally rigid as possible, and the lightweight additional skin should be modified towards the high frequencies (flexurally soft). Due to the sound dispersal of the additional skin, the excitation of the solid wall structure is significantly reduced. Typical additional skins consist of plasterboard or gypsum fibreboard, which are usually fitted in front of the solid wall using metal studs. Ideally, the additional skin is installed freestanding in front of the solid wall. > Fig. 38

○ **Note**: The resonance frequency f_0 should be as low as possible ($f_0 \leq 80$ Hz). In order to fully account for the coincidence frequency, the board thickness should be limited to between 12.5 mm and 18 mm. Where greater mass is required, an additional lining layer should be applied.

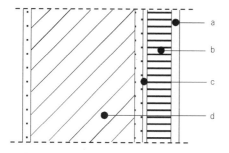

a = Plasterboard or gypsum
    fibreboard
b = Mineral insulation
c = Air gap
d = Existing brickwork with layer
    of plaster

Fig. 38: Diagram of solid wall with additional skin

IMPACT SOUND INSULATION

As a rule, the mass per square area of loadbearing concrete floor slabs, stair runs, and landings, and also that of a loadbearing timber floor, is not sufficient to achieve adequate underline impact sound insulation. In order to meet the requirements for impact sound insulation, these elements have to be upgraded with additional measures, such as a floating screed with impact sound insulation or impact-sound-reducing elastic bearing pads.

For the purpose of improving underline impact sound insulation, additional layers of floor finishes floating on an elastic material (floating screeds) have proven useful. An example is cement-based screed floating on a layer of impact sound insulation material. In residential construction, such floating screeds are usually placed on impact sound insulation material consisting of expanded polystyrene (EPS) or mineral insulation. The most important criterion for selecting impact sound insulation is the dynamic stiffness. This describes the behaviour of the material under changing loads, for example, when walking on a floor between two storeys. The lower the flexural rigidity, the better the impact sound insulation of the building component. However, in order to ensure that the screed slab is not subject to excessive deformation, the selected impact sound insulation material should comply with the load assumptions in the structural calculations. > Fig. 39   ○

Impact sound
insulation

○ **Note**: It is questionable whether soft-impact floor finishes on their own, such as fitted carpets, are adequate for reducing impact sound transmission owing to the fact that they may have to be replaced over time. As a rule, users should be able to select a floor finish of their choice.

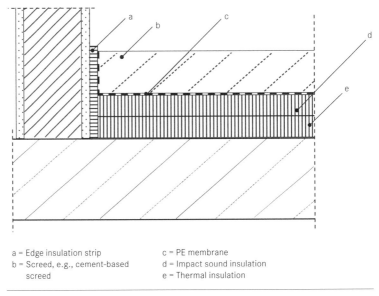

a = Edge insulation strip
b = Screed, e.g., cement-based
    screed

c = PE membrane
d = Impact sound insulation
e = Thermal insulation

Fig. 39: Example of a floating screed with edge connection

The construction with a screed, impact sound insulation, and the loadbearing floor slab forms a double-skin structure and can be considered a <u>mass-spring-mass system</u>. In this case, the impact sound insulation serves as the spring and reduces the transmission of sound energy to the loadbearing element. It is important here, as in the case of the airborne sound insulation of double-skin wall structures, that – as a minimum requirement – the resonance frequency is lower than the range relevant to building acoustics. The resonance frequency and hence the quality of the impact sound insulation can be influenced by modifying the mass of the screed and of the loadbearing floor slab, as well as by choosing the rigidity of the impact sound insulation material.

In view of the fact that loadbearing timber floors have significantly less mass per square area compared to those in solid construction, it is usually necessary to add additional mass to the loadbearing floor. This can take the form of heavy loose material (approx. bulk density $\delta \geq 1{,}500$ kg/m^3), of small-format concrete slabs (approx. 30 x 30 cm), or of the combination of timber with concrete in the construction. The combination of timber with concrete has the advantage that the added mass can also be utilized for the loadbearing capacity. > Fig. 40

A prerequisite for adequate impact sound insulation is that the floating screed is installed without structure-borne sound bridges. > Fig. 41 This means that the screed must not have any direct contact with the structural floor, the walls, or any penetrating components. The impact sound insula-

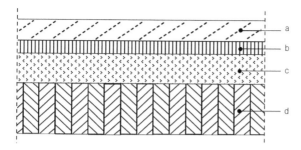

a = Screed
b = Mineral impact sound insulation
    material; s' ≤ 9 MN/m³
c = Bulk mass, e.g., stone chippings
    with bulk density ≥ 1,500 kg/m²
d = Solid timber floor

Fig. 40: Timber floor construction with added mass

tion material must be placed without gaps, and a PE membrane must be laid between the screed and the insulation material. Edge insulation strips are used to separate the screed from vertical components; again, these must be installed along the walls or around columns without any gaps. Furthermore, it is important to ensure that the floor finish supported by the floating screed has no direct contact with adjacent building components. ○

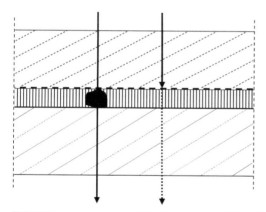

Fig. 41: Floating screed with structure-borne sound bridge

○ **Note**: As a rule, the structural floors in solid construction have a significantly greater mass than those in lightweight and timber construction. In order to deal adequately with the resonance frequency in such structures, the impact sound insulation material used must have a significantly lower dynamic stiffness s', for example, mineral insulation material with a dynamic stiffness s' of between 6 and 9 MN/m³.

○ **Note**: In solid construction buildings, it is common to use polyethylene (PE) edge insulation strips; in lightweight or timber construction buildings, with their lower mass, the edge insulation strips used normally consist of mineral insulation material.

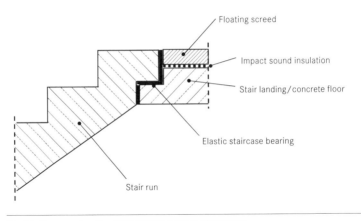

Floating screed

Impact sound insulation

Stair landing/concrete floor

Elastic staircase bearing

Stair run

Fig. 42: Diagram showing elastic bearing at top of stair run

Impact sound – staircases

As a rule, structure-borne sound insulation elements are used to reduce the impact sound of stair runs. These elements are placed underneath the stair run, where they rest on the floor and intermediate landing. This is assuming that the stair run is not in direct contact with the walls of the stairwell. It is also possible to use structure-borne sound insulation elements to connect the stair landing to the loadbearing walls and floors of the stairwell. In view of the fact that there is likely to be greater impact sound transmission from stair landings to the adjacent rooms, these landings are usually also finished with a floating screed. > Fig. 42

SERVICES INSTALLATIONS

Services installations are fixed installations such as water installations (WCs, showers, washbasins, etc.), heating and ventilation systems, elevators, or a plant in commercial premises. The noise from these installations is generated by fixings and the flow of water (including wastewater); this structure-borne sound is transmitted via the pipe walls and pipe fixings to the building fabric (walls, floors, etc.) and is then dispersed into the space as airborne sound.

Measures to reduce the noise pollution from services installations

In order to protect the residents and/or users of a building from the noise pollution generated by services installations, a range of different measures should be considered at the design stage. In the first instance, the fixings selected should have low-noise emission characteristics (e.g., low-noise fixings, sanitary tapware class I).

In addition, the layout plans can be designed such that sanitary rooms are not directly adjacent to rooms requiring noise protection. For example, in terms of horizontal arrangement, sanitary rooms can be placed next to a room that does not require noise protection; in terms

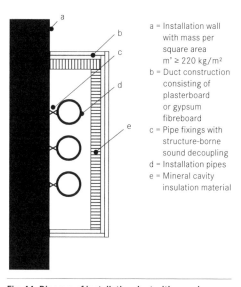

a = Installation wall with mass per square area m' ≥ 220 kg/m²
b = Duct construction consisting of plasterboard or gypsum fibreboard
c = Pipe fixings with structure-borne sound decoupling
d = Installation pipes
e = Mineral cavity insulation material

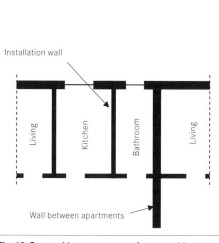

Installation wall

Living

Kitchen

Bathroom

Living

Wall between apartments

Fig. 43: Favourable arrangement of rooms with installations

Fig. 44: Diagram of installation duct with sound insulation

of vertical arrangement, this principle should be applied accordingly. Furthermore, it makes sense to arrange the sanitary rooms back to back with a kitchen, with both rooms sharing a separating wall. > Fig. 43

In addition to the layout design, the mass per square area of the in-stallation wall has a major impact on the noise emitted by installations. The greater the mass of the installation wall, the less it can be excited and the lower the installation noises. The airborne sound emitted by in-stallation pipes can be reduced by adding an extra layer of drywall to the construction. This creates an installation duct, which needs to be ade-quately insulated with mineral insulation material on two sides in order to prevent reflection and resonance in the cavity. > Fig. 44

Installation wall and installation duct

O

○ **Note**: In order to reduce the structure-borne sound excitation from installation noises as much as possible, the installation wall should have a mass per square area of at least 220 kg/m².

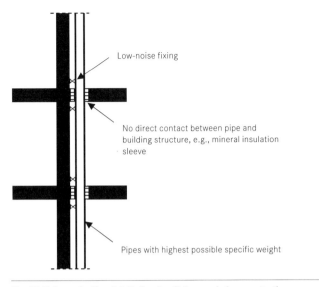

Low-noise fixing

No direct contact between pipe and
building structure, e.g., mineral insulation
sleeve

Pipes with highest possible specific weight

Fig. 45: Noise reduction details for pipe fixings and pipe penetrations

Installation pipes

These days, <u>installation pipes</u> are not installed under plaster, which requires the insertion of unfavourable channels, recesses, and openings in the masonry; instead, they are installed in ducts or covered by an additional drywall layer. In order to reduce the structure-borne sound transmission of the fixtures (e.g., washbasin, WC, bathtub, shower tray, etc.), they should be installed with low-noise fixing sets. Similarly, pipes should be installed with low-noise fixings (e.g., pipe clips with rubber inserts), and it is imperative that, where a pipe penetrates a building component, direct contact between the pipe and the building fabric is avoided. In order to reduce the vibrations caused by water falling in wastewater pipes, these pipes should have a high specific weight. > Fig. 45

Ventilation and
heating aggregates

The ventilation and heating of buildings often require the installation of larger technical aggregates (ventilation plant, combined heat and power units, etc.). In order to prevent the transmission of structure-borne sound to rooms requiring noise protection, it is normally necessary, in addition to the sound reduction measures of the pipe installation described above, to place the respective aggregate on elastic bearing pads. In view of the fact that such a plant is usually installed separately in a plant room or on the roof, it is important to ensure at the design stage that no rooms requiring noise protection are located directly adjacent, beneath, or above. Likewise, pipework leading to and from the plant should be installed along routes through rooms that do not require noise protection.

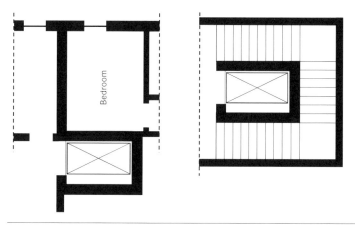

Bedroom

Fig. 46: Unfavourable arrangement of an elevator shaft next to a room requiring noise protection (left); favourable arrangement of an elevator shaft integrated into the stairwell (right)

The principle of locating sanitary rooms in the plan layout also applies to <u>elevator shafts</u>, which should not be directly adjacent to rooms requiring noise protection. > Fig. 46

Elevator shaft

Depending on the location of the elevator shaft in the building, the mass per square area of the shaft wall and that of adjacent and flanking building components must be sufficiently great. Furthermore, the elevator and the elevator motor must be attached to the loadbearing structure using elastic elements in order to reduce the transmission of structure-borne sound.

SOUND PROTECTION – EXTERNAL BUILDING COMPONENTS

The measures needed to reduce noise transmitted through external building components depend on the noise pollution in the environment and on the function of the respective room. Sound protection measures required at the external facade depend on the construction of the external elements, such as walls, roof, windows, roller shutter boxes, and any penetrations in these (e.g., wall and window vents). As a rule, the most critical parts of the facade are the windows, roller shutter boxes, and any penetrating elements.

<u>Windows</u> are needed to admit sufficient daylight to the room and to provide enough fresh air when opened. These requirements have an adverse effect on a construction that would optimize sound reduction. It is also important to remember that openable window casements require seals to prevent unwanted drafts. To achieve adequate sound reduction, such opening casements need to be designed to close with adequate compacting pressure.

Windows

The glass used in windows can consist of single, double, or triple glazing, as well as safety glass, such as laminated safety glass. Owing to current energy conservation requirements, residential and commercial buildings are usually fitted with double or triple glazing.

The sound reduction provided by single glazing and laminated safety glass primarily depends on the mass per square area of the respective pane. Laminated safety glass consisting of two or more panes with a protective film between the panes does not have a positive effect on sound reduction, due to the coincidence effect, unless somewhat thicker glass panes are used. Owing to the fact that the individual panes are bonded together, laminated safety glass is less flexurally rigid compared to toughened safety glass of equal thickness.

Double glazing units have a gap between the two glass panes. The sound reduction effect of double or triple glazing depends on the mass per square area of the individual panes and the distance between the panes. Where this distance is too small, the sound reduction is not any greater compared to single glazing of equal mass per square area; it may even be worse owing to the relatively high resonance frequency. Compared to single glazing, an improvement can't be achieved unless the distance between the panes in the double glazing is at least approx. 16 mm. > Fig. 47

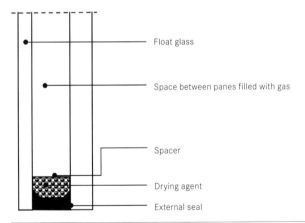

Float glass

Space between panes filled with gas

Spacer

Drying agent

External seal

Fig. 47: Diagram of double glazing unit

○ **Note**: Laminated safety glass does not have a sound reduction advantage, compared to single glazing, unless it is at least 6 mm thick.

In order to achieve the best possible sound insulation of the double glazing (insulating glazing unit), the two panes should have different critical coincidence frequencies. This is achieved by selecting panes of different thicknesses.

As a rule, the material of the window frame does not play a role in the sound reduction of the window; the sound reduction index achievable is the same for wood, plastic, and metal windows. However, the detailing of the connecting joints between the window and the adjacent building fabric (wall, floor, ceiling), as well as the detailing of the functional joints (joints between window frame and casement frame), play an important role in the sound reduction of a window. The cavity in the connecting joint between window frame and building fabric must be fully filled with insulation material (mineral insulation, foam insulation, etc.). Depending on the sound insulation requirements for the window, it is recommended to insert a permanently elastic compound into both sides of the joint. The functional joint can be sealed by fitting two- or three-layer profile seals at different levels in order to improve the sound reduction properties. In addition to the number of seals, adequate compacting pressure is required in order to achieve the stipulated sound reduction.

Room acoustics

In room acoustics, the engineer endeavours to optimize the audibility in a room. The acoustic quality of a room plays an important role in making speech understandable and in the transmission of musical performances. Furthermore, good room acoustics design reduces undesirable sound in a room. The important parameters affecting the acoustic quality of a room are the geometry of the room, the volume (primary structure), and the detailing of the component surfaces and furniture and fixings (secondary structure). Other important factors are the placement of the room in the building, the sound reduction properties of building components enclosing the room, and any noise created by services installations.

The room acoustics requirements vary according to the function of the room. Ideally, teaching premises and auditoria should have acoustic properties that allow speech to be clearly audible throughout. Rooms for musical performances should be designed to ensure that the sound of music can fully unfold. In open-plan offices and, for example, at bank counters, audibility should be as good as possible over short distances; however, even at a slightly increased distance, as little as possible of what is spoken should be audible.

KEY ROOM ACOUSTICS VARIABLES

In order to explain the analytical methods used in room acoustics, we will first explain the principles of sound absorption and reverberation time in terms of basic physics.

Sound absorption coefficient, equivalent sound absorption surface

The sound absorption coefficient indicates the proportion of sound energy hitting the surface of an object. It is stated as a value without unit of between 0 (= no absorption) and 1 (= full absorption). As a rule, the sound absorption coefficient is determined in a suitable reverberation room using a standardized procedure. > Fig. 48

The equivalent sound absorption surface is calculated by multiplying the sound absorption coefficient by the square area impacted by the sound energy. This results in a model surface with full absorption characteristics, which therefore has a sound absorption coefficient of 1. This surface can be imagined as an open window. The equivalent absorption surface of an entire room results from adding all the different partial areas. In addition, the equivalent absorption surface is affected by furniture and fixings, people, curtains, etc.

Reverberation time

In room acoustics, the reverberation time is the most important criterion. This is defined as the time taken for the sound level in a room to drop by 60 dB after the source of the sound has been switched off or after a sufficiently loud signal has been generated. > Fig. 49

Fig. 48: Reverberation room of the Fraunhofer Institute for Building Physics IBP in Stuttgart

In simple rooms, the reverberation time can be calculated using Sabine's reverberation equation:

$$T = 0.163 \times \frac{V}{A}$$

whereby:
V = room volume in m³
A = equivalent sound absorption coefficient in m²

○ **Note**: Part of the sound energy entering the absorber is changed into heat (dissipation) and another part penetrates the building component via the absorber (transmission).

○ **Note**: When using Sabine's reverberation equation to perform this calculation, only the room volume and the equivalent absorption surface are taken into account, not special shapes of the room or any reflections from the walls that prolong reverberation. When doing this calculation for larger rooms and rooms with more complex geometries, it is therefore recommended to use a 3D calculation program.

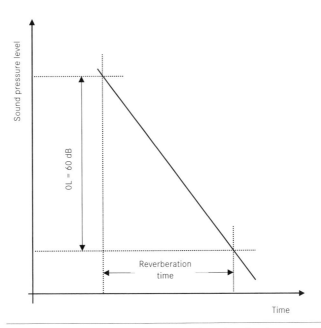

Fig. 49: Decay curve representing the measured reverberation time

In closed rooms, it is important to note that, owing to sound reflection at the confining surfaces of the room, the decay of sound pressure is, within a certain distance, independent of the location of the source of the sound. This area is referred to as the <u>direct sound field</u> and depends on the <u>reverberation radius</u>. Within this reverberation radius, the proportion of direct sound predominates. In the area of the reverberation radius, the proportions of <u>direct sound</u> and of <u>diffuse sound</u> are equal. The area beyond the reverberation radius is referred to as the <u>diffuse sound field</u>; here, direct sound and reflected sound are superposed. The sound level in the diffuse sound field depends on the absorption properties of

○ ■ the room. > Fig. 50

○ **Note**: The reverberation radius depends on the <u>equivalent absorption surface</u> and can be calculated as follows:

$$r_h = \sqrt{\frac{A}{16 \times \pi}}$$

whereby:
A = equivalent degree of sound absorption

■ **Tip**: When designing the acoustics of a room and deciding where room acoustics measures should be employed, it is important to determine the reverberation radius because sound-absorbing measures are not effective when placed within that radius.

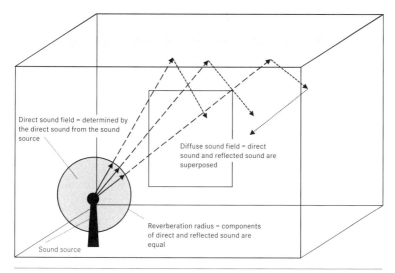

Fig. 50: Direct sound field, reverberation radius, diffuse sound field

Other key variables for assessing the acoustic quality of a room are the <u>distinctiveness</u> and <u>clarity</u>, as well as the <u>speech transmission index (STI)</u>. The measure of distinctiveness is used to assess the clarity of speech and how easy it is to distinguish syllables. The measure of clarity describes the transparency of music. The speech transmission index is a measure of speech intelligibility. This takes into account not only acoustic conditions but also noise interference. The speech transmission index is expressed with a value of between 0 and 1, without unit of measure. Table 5 shows the degree of speech intelligibility to be expected for the respective speech transmission index (STI).

○

○ **Note**: The STI is used for assessing loudspeaker systems used in, for example, airports, railway stations, department stores, and schools. In these buildings, it is necessary to achieve adequate audibility and speech intelligibility, for example, for information on evacuation in the case of an emergency. It is of critical importance that consonants be understood because these form the syllable and give meaning to the word. For this reason, the speech transmission index recommended for teaching premises is > 0.75.

STI	Speech intelligibility
0–0.3	inadequate
0.3–0.45	poor
0.45–0.5	adequate
0.6–0.75	good
0.75–1.0	excellent

SOUND PROPAGATION IN ROOMS

In contrast to the propagation of sound in the open, where the sound pressure level decreases with increasing distance, sound in rooms is subject to reflection and multiple reflection from the room-confining surfaces, which results in a diffuse sound field. From a certain minimum distance from the sound source, the sound pressure level is nearly independent of the location of the source. Depending on the room geometry and the absorption behaviour of the room-confining surfaces, there will either be reflections or, in rooms with many absorbing surfaces, quick absorption of the sound power. This has an effect on the intensity of the sound pressure in the diffuse sound field.

ROOM ACOUSTICS MEASURES

The design of room acoustics measures usually relies on sound-absorbing materials. In rooms with sources of noise, such as industrial premises, workshops, restaurants, etc., these measures are used to attenuate noise and reduce the sound pressure level. In rooms that require good room acoustics, for example, classrooms, lecture halls, etc., sound absorbers are used to manage reverberation time as well as to reduce sound reflections. Nowadays, in practice, a distinction is made between porous absorbers and resonance or panel absorbers. > Fig. 51

Porous absorbers   Porous absorbers are used for sound absorption of a wide range of primarily high and medium frequencies. Porous absorbers include, for example, acoustic plasters, fibre insulation materials, plastic foam, and acoustic curtains. In acoustic absorbers, the sound energy is converted to thermal energy through friction. A prerequisite for this is that the sound energy penetrates as deeply as possible into the material. This means that the material should be as open-pored as possible and that its air volume should be as large as possible compared to the total volume. When selecting a porous absorber, it is important to note its flow resistivity, which is a measure of its resistance to the penetrating sound energy. If the flow resistivity is too great, the sound can't penetrate the material sufficiently. If the resistivity is too low, the sound passes through the material and is reflected from the surface behind.

Fig. 51: Porous absorber (acoustic plaster)

In addition to the material properties and dimensions of the porous absorber, the arrangement of the absorber in the room is also important. The sound energy is reduced through friction. This friction loss is greatest where the air particles move fastest. For this reason, porous absorbers must have a certain thickness or must be placed at a certain distance from a reflecting wall or ceiling surface in the area of the speed maximum. In view of the fact that the wavelength λ of airborne sound waves varies a great deal (low-pitched sounds have long wavelengths; high-pitched sounds have short wavelengths), the distance required depends on the frequency of the sound to be absorbed. > Fig. 52

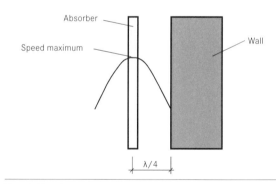

Fig. 52: Absorber, e.g., curtain in the area of the speed maximum

O **Note**: In order to ensure that the sound energy impacting on sound-absorbing material, such as mineral insulation, is adequately absorbed, the flow resistivity should be selected to be between 5 kPa s/m and 40 kPa s/m.

Low frequencies can be absorbed using <u>panel resonators</u>, which usually consist of thin, non-perforated panels, such as wood-based and plasterboard panels mounted to the substrate such that a cavity is formed. In order to increase the sound-absorbing effect of panel resonators, the cavity can be filled with mineral insulation material. The panels are mounted to the ceiling or wall using wood or metal mountings. This method of fixing must allow the panel to vibrate freely. The solid panel and the enclosed cavity form a mass-spring system that has its greatest effect in the range of the resonance frequency. The resonance frequency of a solid panel depends on the weight of the panel and the depth of the cavity. > Fig. 53

In addition to panel resonators with solid panels, it is possible to use resonators with perforated panels; the perforations may be evenly distributed round holes, square holes, or slots. These are <u>perforated panel resonators</u>. Depending on the required absorption function, perforated panel resonators can be varied in terms of panel weight, depth of cavity, and the proportion of apertures. > Fig. 54 and 55

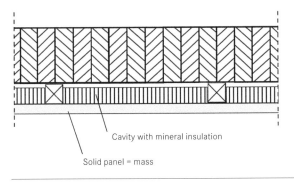

Cavity with mineral insulation

Solid panel = mass

Fig. 53: Panel resonator/perforated panel resonators

O **Note**: In order to ensure that the panel vibrates freely, the mounting devices must be spaced as far apart as possible. The distance between mounting devices should be at least 0.5 m and the freely vibrating area should be approx. 0.4 m².

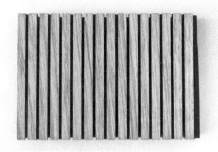

Fig. 54: Perforated panel resonator/"open panel" resonator

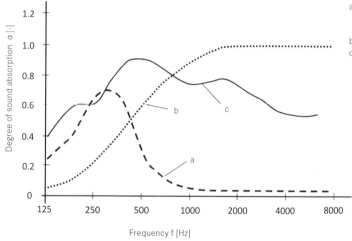

a = Panel absorber with solid surface and mineral insulation in cavity
b = Porous absorber
c = Example of a perforated panel absorber with 8 mm hole diameter, an aperture proportion of 19% and a cavity depth of approx. 220 mm

Fig. 55: Typical frequency curves of porous absorbers and panel absorbers

Helmholtz resonators can be used to augment or to absorb sound. Helmholtz resonators Well-known examples of devices that augment sound are string instruments. For example, in an acoustic guitar the sound is augmented by the body of the guitar with its aperture. In this case, the mass of the air in the sound hole (<u>resonator neck</u>) and the air enclosed in the cavity behind form a mass-spring system. In order to absorb the sound and reduce its energy as much as possible, mineral insulation material is inserted in the cavity and a fleece is inserted in the resonator aperture. Helmholtz

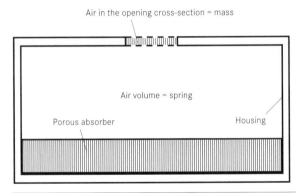

Air in the opening cross-section = mass

Air volume = spring

Porous absorber

Housing

Fig. 56: Function of Helmholtz resonators

resonators are often used to absorb individual low frequencies, something that requires a space with a large volume. > Fig. 56

ROOM ACOUSTICS REQUIREMENTS

The objective in the design of room acoustics is to ensure that the expectations of the listeners are met. The requirements and the assessment of general function rooms, such as teaching rooms, lecture halls, meeting rooms, offices, etc., are mainly based on reverberation time. A frequent distinction is made between rooms requiring good audibility across medium and large distances (classrooms, auditoria, etc.) and rooms requiring good audibility across shorter distances, such as offices, booking halls, and libraries.

Rooms requiring good audibility across medium and large distances

Good audibility across medium and large distances can be achieved by managing the reverberation time associated with the respective type of function, taking into account the volume of the space and using appropriately placed sound-absorbing and sound-directing measures. As a rule, the required values for reverberation time are specified in national standards. Table 6 lists optimal reverberation times for everyday rooms with common space volumes.

Music teaching rooms and music rehearsal rooms need a rather extended reverberation time, although the actual requirement largely depends on the respective activity taking place. Music rooms used for teaching singing require a longer reverberation time in order to ensure that the sound can better unfold, whereas in teaching rooms, for example, for drumming, the reverberation time should be rather shorter because greater sound attenuation is required due to the sound intensity. In consequence, in music teaching rooms for different instruments it is desirable to aim for variability in reverberation time. This can be achieved, for

Table. 6: Optimal reverberation time depending on function of room

Function of room	Optimal reverberation time at 1,000 Hz
Teaching room	0.4–0.6 s
Auditorium	0.9–1.1 s
Conference and meeting room	0.4–0.6 s
Music practice room	0.4–0.8 s
Gymnasium	1.2–1.4 s

example, by using appropriate acoustic curtains in front of the wall surfaces that can be opened and closed.

The acoustics in rooms with special audibility requirements, such as concert halls and theatres, requires dedicated design by a specialist. Table 7 lists a few approximate values for optimal reverberation times in rooms for speech-based and musical performances.

Rooms for speech and communication, in particular for persons with limited hearing ability, require high direct sound transmission from the speaker to the listener and a reduction in the reverberation time and in the reflections that extend reverberation time. In addition, interference noise from outside (road traffic, industrial noise, etc.), from neighbouring rooms, or via ventilation outlets should be reduced as much as possible. In order to achieve adequate audibility, interference noise should be at least 10 dB under the transmission level. Depending on the function of the room, the maximum sound levels of interference noises shown in Table 8 are recommended.

Interference noise level

Table 7: Approximate values for optimal reverberation times in concert halls and theatres

Room function	Optimal reverberation time at 1,000 Hz
Speech-based theatre	0.7–0.9 s
Musical performance (chamber music)	0.9–1.4 s
Musical performance (opera)	1.2–1.6 s
Musical performance (concert)	1.7–2.1 s
Organ music	2.3–2.7 s

Table 8: Maximum values for interference noise levels

Type of function	Max. interference noise level
Music rooms, conservatories	≤ 30 dB(A)
Rooms for speech, lectures, teaching	≤ 35 dB(A)
Sports facilities, sports halls	≤ 40 dB(A)

Table 9: Volume indicator k depending on function of room

Function of room	Volume indicator k [m³/place]
Speech-based rooms (e.g., seminar rooms)	3–5
Auditoria, speech-based theatres	4–6
Multipurpose halls for speech and music	5–8
Musical theatres	5–8
Concert halls	7–12

Volume indicator

When designing rooms for speech-based or musical performances, the room volume should be adjusted to the number of anticipated people/places. Table 9 shows the volume indicator k that should be aimed for, depending on the function of the room.

If the volume indicator is too high in rooms for speech-based performances, it may be necessary to install additional room acoustics measures owing to the extended reverberation time. By contrast, volume indicators that are too low can be a disadvantage in rooms used for musical performances owing to the reduced reverberation time. In such cases, it is usually quite difficult to correct the acoustics.

Rooms for audibility across a short distance

In rooms requiring audibility across a short distance, the respective room acoustics properties are achieved by installing appropriate acoustics-damping devices. These properties can be assessed, for example, by establishing the ratio of equivalent sound absorption surface to room volume.

The design of the room acoustics in open-plan offices requires special measures. On the one hand, communication between members of staff must not present any problems; on the other hand, such communication should not cause interference. This calls not only for adequate damping devices but also for sound-screening elements (such as partition screens) in order to reduce direct sound from one workplace to another.

■ **Tip**: Practical experience shows that even with optimal design of the room acoustics in open-plan offices, users are frequently discontent. The reason for this is usually that the individual workspaces are arranged too close together. If it is not possible to reduce the density of workspaces, it may be possible to address the situation by raising the level of background noise, referred to as sound masking.

ACOUSTIC DESIGN OF ROOMS

From an acoustics design point of view, there is no optimal solution Primary structure regarding the design of the <u>primary structure</u> of a room. However, certain geometric shapes, such as circular and elliptical plan layouts, have a positive or negative effect on the room acoustics, depending on the function of the room. The design of rooms for speech-based and musical performances should primarily aim to provide the listener with adequate <u>direct sound</u> and <u>first reflections</u>. This presupposes that the speaker or the orchestra is surrounded by adequate reflective surfaces. In rooms or halls for speech-based performances, a wide room layout is advantageous in order to keep the distance between speakers and listeners as short as possible. By contrast, in rooms used for musical performances, narrow, rectangular room layouts in the shape of a <u>shoe box</u> are particularly suitable as this will ensure that the rows at the back are provided with adequate side-wall reflections. This means that the stage must be placed at the short side of the room.

It is also possible to <u>raise seats</u> in order to ensure that adequate direct sound reaches the listeners. Where this is not possible for functional reasons, it is also possible to arrange for the performers to act on a raised platform or stage. > Fig. 57

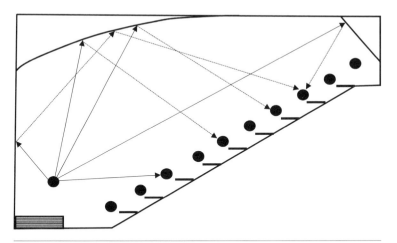

Fig. 57: Diagram of an auditorium with raised seating

In <u>circular</u> and <u>elliptical plan layouts,</u> as well as in rooms with <u>curved wall and ceiling surfaces,</u> it is possible that undesirable sound concentration occurs. On the other hand, it is also possible to use curved surfaces deliberately to supply the audience with reflected sound. > Fig. 58

In the case of a circular plan layout, it is possible that multiple reflections occur along the wall due to <u>grazing sound incidence,</u> i.e., when the speaker stands close to the wall and speaks in a direction parallel to the wall. This phenomenon is referred to as a <u>whispering gallery</u> because even quiet speech can be heard at the opposite wall due to multiple
● reflections along the wall. > Fig. 59

Secondary structure The term "secondary structure" refers to the acoustic devices and finishes applied to walls and ceilings. The transmission of a signal from a speaker to a listener, i.e., room acoustics, is influenced by geometric
○ and diffuse reflections as well as by absorbing materials.

Where <u>reverberative walls are arranged in parallel,</u> there is a risk of <u>flutter echoes</u> occurring. These can be reduced by placing the wall at a slightly oblique angle of approx. 5° or by attaching sound-absorbing materials on the respective opposite wall. > Fig. 61

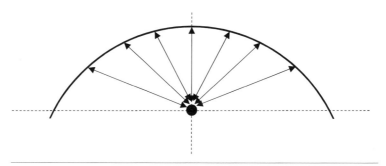

Fig. 58: Concentration of sound as a result of sound reflected from a circular surface

● **Example**: A well-known example of a whispering gallery is the dome of St Paul's Cathedral in London.

○ **Note**: In rooms intended for speech-based events, the delay between the time when the direct sound arrives at the listener and when the reflected sound first arrives there should not be more than max. 50 ms. In terms of physical distance, this means that the long path of the reflections should not be more than 17 m longer than the short path of the direct sound. > Fig. 60

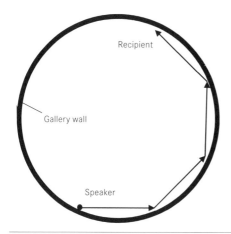

Fig. 59: Whispering gallery effect

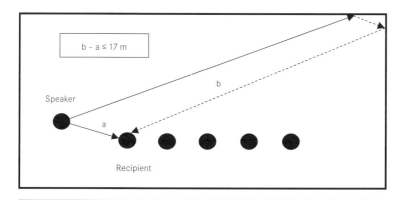

Fig. 60: Diagram showing the short path of the direct sound from the speaker to the recipient (a) and the long path of the reflected sound from the speaker to the recipient (b); the long path should not be more than 17 m longer than the short path

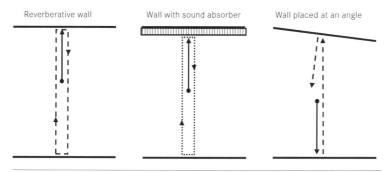

Fig. 61: Flutter echoes and measures for reducing them

For the arrangement of acoustically effective surfaces in everyday rooms, it is preferable to consider the ceiling as the first step in order to achieve even distribution across the room. In rooms just requiring effective damping, it is best to apply the acoustics measures to the entire ceiling. If there is only scant furniture in the room, there is a risk that flutter echoes can form due to reflection from the reverberative wall surfaces. This can be stopped by applying additional acoustically effective surfaces to the walls.

In rooms requiring a high degree of speech intelligibility (teaching rooms, lecture halls, etc.), the middle area of the ceiling should be kept reverberative, i.e., without sound-absorbing devices. This has the advantage that speech also reaches the back rows due to reflection from this reverberative area. In addition, some parts of the wall opposite the speaker should be fitted with sound-absorbing materials in order to avoid unwanted sound reflections impacting on the listeners and also on the speaker (this applies to rooms longer than 9 m). As an alternative to absorbing materials, it is possible to place reflectors at oblique angles in front of the back wall. These have the advantage of helping to direct the sound energy to the back rows. Sound-absorbing surfaces at the side walls next to the speaker, at the wall behind the speaker, or on the ceiling above the speaker should be avoided so that the sound energy is not reduced unnecessarily. These surfaces should be sound reflective at the medium and higher frequencies; if appropriate, a low-frequency-absorbing device should be fitted to these areas. > Fig. 62

The installation of a fitted carpet as the only acoustics measure will not have the desired effect because as a rule this will only absorb tones in the higher frequency range. Installing a fitted carpet may nevertheless be useful because this will eliminate unwanted sounds, such as those
○ from chairs being moved across the floor.

○ **Note**: The arrangement of sound-absorbing devices shown above is suitable for teaching rooms in the classical layout (with the teacher at the front). Where teaching in a teaching room takes place in an "open" manner, the undamped area of the ceiling should be covered.

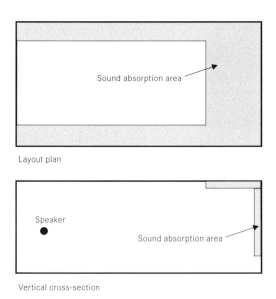

Layout plan

Vertical cross-section

Fig. 62: Effective arrangement of sound-absorbing devices for rooms used for speech

INCLUSION AND BARRIER FREEDOM IN ACOUSTICS

The subject of barrier freedom in acoustics is becoming more prominent, especially in the design of teaching rooms and lecture halls, as well
as conference and meeting rooms. For people with impaired hearing, with
reduced concentration ability and attention deficit, and with a migration
background, the quality of the room acoustics and hence the speech intelligibility can be critical. For rooms used for teaching and speech-based
activities, which are intended to be inclusive of all listeners, it is recommended to ensure that the reverberation time is reduced by 20 per cent.
This reduction in the reverberation time should relate to the range between 250 and 2,000 Hz, i.e., the octave bands of speech. This not only
results in better speech intelligibility but also users benefit from a lower
interference noise level, which means that the speaker can reduce his/
her voice volume, which in turn means less effort.   ○

○ **Note**: The higher the interference noise level, the
louder the speaker has to speak. This causes an additional increase in the sound level. This "ratcheting up"
of the sound level is also referred to as the Lombard
effect.

MEASURING REVERBERATION TIME

As mentioned in the previous chapters, the reverberation time can be calculated; in addition, it is possible to determine this by measuring. For this purpose, a broadband signal is generated in the respective room or, in the case of simple measurements, an impulse is generated. Once the sound source has been switched off, the decay process is recorded. The signal generated must be distinctly distinguishable from the background noise level. The sound source to be used can be a loudspeaker with a spherical radiation characteristic (e.g., a dodecahedron > Fig. 63). It is important to ensure that the loudspeaker and the measuring microphone are placed at minimum distances from the floor, the ceiling, and the surrounding walls. In addition, there must be a minimum distance between the loudspeaker and the measuring microphone, which is governed by standards.

Fig. 63: Dodecahedron loudspeaker

Summary

This volume conveys the essential background knowledge of the many fields of sound protection. The subjects described are intended to raise students' awareness of the many issues involved so that they will take sound protection into account in the design of buildings and building components at an early stage.

At the early design stages, the orientation of a building and its plan layout can be chosen to favourably affect noise protection. The design of external facades should take conceptual, structural, energy-related, and fire protection aspects into account, as well as parameters relating to sound protection.

In the design of the plan layout of the building, internal sound protection can be taken into account by avoiding the arrangement of loud rooms directly adjacent to rooms requiring sound protection. Readers are also familiarized with the options for the design of building components that help to optimize internal sound protection, as well as with the sound-related properties inherent in such components.

Furthermore, regarding the design of rooms requiring good audibility, readers are shown suitable options for the design of room geometries and the selection of materials to meet the acoustics requirements resulting from the planned use of the room. A good acoustics performance in a room also depends on where acoustic devices are placed, and this is covered in another section.

Appendix

BIBLIOGRAPHY

DIN 4109-1:2018-01 Sound insulation in buildings – Part 1: Minimum requirements, Beuth Verlag GmbH; date: 2018

DIN 4109-1:2018-01 Sound insulation in buildings – Part 2: Verification of compliance with the requirements by calculation, Beuth Verlag GmbH; date: 2018

DIN 18041:2016-03 Acoustic quality in rooms – Specifications and instructions for the room acoustic design, Beuth Verlag GmbH; date: 2016

DIN 18005-1:2002-07 Noise abatement in town planning: Fundamentals and directions for planning, Beuth Verlag GmbH; date: 2002

W. Fasold, E. Veres: Schallschutz + Raumakustik in der Praxis: Planungsbeispiele und konstruktive Lösungen, Verlag für Bauwesen, Berlin; Stand: 2003

W. Fasold, E. Sonntag, H. Winkler: Bau- und Raumakustik, VEB Verlag für Bauwesen, Berlin; Stand: 1987

Informationsdienst Holz: Holzbauhandbuch-Reihe 3. Teil, 3. Folge, Holzbau Deutschland-Institut e. V. Berlin; Stand: 2019

C. Nocke: Everyday room acoustics: Hearing, planning, understanding. Stuttgart: IRB Fraunhofer; date: 2019

E. Sälzer, G. Eßer, J. Maack, T. Möck, M. Sahl: Schallschutz im Hochbau – Grundbegriffe, Anforderungen, Konstruktionen, Nachweise, Ernst & Sohn, Berlin; Stand: 2014

VDI 2720 Blatt 1:1997-03 Noise control by barriers outdoors, Beuth Verlag GmbH; date: 1997

W. M. Willems, K. Schild, D. Stricker: Schallschutz: Bauakustik. Grundlagen – Luftschallschutz – Trittschallschutz, Springer Vieweg, Wiesbaden; Stand: 2012

FIGURES

Figure 14: Wikimedia Commons File:Ear-anatomy-text-small-zh.svg
Figure 48: © Fraunhofer Institute for Building Physics IBP
Figure 52: Reverberation room of the Fraunhofer IBP in Stuttgart
All other Figures: Produced by the author

Editor of the series: Bert Blelefeld
Concept: Bert Bielefeld, Annette Gref
Copy editing: Patricia Kot
Project coordination: Annette Gref
Production: Amelie Solbrig
Layout and cover design: Andreas Hidber
Typesetting: Sven Schrape

Paper: Magno Natural, 120 g/m²
Printed by: Beltz Grafische Betriebe GmbH,
Bad Langensalza

Library of Congress Control Number:
2021931157

Bibliographical information of the German
National Library
The German National Library registers this
publication in the German National Bibliography;
detailed bibliographical data can be found on
the Internet via http://dnb.dnb.de.

ISBN 978-3-0356-2103-7
e-ISBN (PDF) 978-3-0356-2201-0
e-ISBN (EPUB) 978-3-0356-2206-5
German Print-ISBN 978-3-0356-2102-0

© 2021 Birkhäuser Verlag GmbH, Basel
PO Box 44, 4009 Basel, Switzerland
A company of Walter de Gruyter GmbH,
Berlin/Boston

9 8 7 6 5 4 3 2 1
www.birkhauser.com